Acknowledgement

The book *Mix it with the Arts* is very close to my heart. The book is based on facts, theories, and my personal experiences and experiments. This book would have been impossible without the constant support of Mr. Awart Kartiyar, who helped me in writing this book from the concept stage to the readable stage. I would like to extend my heartfelt gratitude to my creative editor, Shubhangi Gupta. Her exceptional talent in creating handmade comics and her invaluable contributions, along with Mr Abhishek Gupta, my friend during our brainstorming sessions, have been instrumental in bringing this book to life. I also want to thank Dr. Onkar Singh (Professor at Mechanical Engineering Dept. HBTU, Kanpur, and Ex-Vice-Chancellor of Madan Mohan Malviya University, Gorakhpur) for improvising the book format and for providing me with suitable suggestions to make this book more appealing.

Uttam Sharma

MIX IT WITH THE ARTS

TRANSFORMING INDIA'S EDUCATION SYSTEM FOR THE NEXT PHASE OF RESEARCH AND DEVELOPMENT

UTTAM SHARMA

SHUBHANGI GUPTA

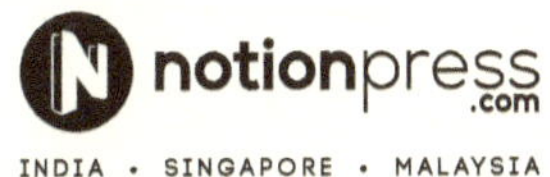

Purpose of the Book

The primary objective of writing the book is to educate people, especially students in schools and colleges who love Science and technology, to follow the S.T.E.A.M. philosophy throughout their lives. Israel spends 4.53 per cent, Sweden spends 3.73 percent, Finland spends 3.45 percent, Japan spends 3.39 percent, and South Korea spends 3.23 percent respectively of their GDP on research.

India invests only 0.9 percent of its GDP on research and is ranked 34th in the world in terms of R&D investment. The numbers reflect the country's state, the level of competitiveness, and the desire to advance in research.

There are various data available related to the global innovation index and artists in the workforce. The strong correlations between the innovation index and the number of artists in the workforce clearly suggest that

Arts make an impact on the country's innovation and GDP.

From enterprises to services and from the private to the public sector, research has impacted every subject.

India is a developing country with numerous problems. Science and technology are critical in determining the best solutions to these issues. The solutions might be published, patented, or even started as a business by the people. India S.T.E.M. Foundation is working hard to educate parents, teachers, and students about the philosophy to create future leaders in India.

S.T.E.A.M. education can create an impact on society by motivating students to become risk-takers, the first and foremost requirement to get out of the comfort zone and deliver exceptional innovation on the ground. Many researchers in India have invested their lives to create impactful products; the same is expected from 21st century India.

This book covers information about various soft skills needed in the 21st century to be leaders in their domains and create an impact by understanding the importance of S.T.E.A.M. This book also highlights the importance of establishing the Dramatics club in schools and colleges to promote Arts education in an experimental way which completes the purpose of

Arts in Science, Technology, Engineering, Arts, and Mathematics (S.T.E.A.M). The book also highlights the importance of research in the 21st century in India.

Maybe this book can help some students understand their purpose of studying Engineering, Science, Technology, and Mathematics better by combining it or mixing it with Arts.

Contents

S.T.E.M vs S.T.E.A.M

An article published in Forbes on 7th Nov 2019 has a bold statement:

"When STEM becomes STEAM, we can change the game."

The article was written by Talia Milgrom Elcott – a graduate of Harvard Business School. The focus of the article was to prepare 100,000 new S.T.E.M teachers in America. The idea of the article was to create more awareness about S.T.E.A.M and create a network of S.T.E.A.M teachers to teach kids of the 21st century the concept of Science, Technology, Engineering, and Mathematics by combining Arts. According to her, every 21st-century job requires creativity, critical thinking, confidence, and collaboration.

In one of her posts, Dr. Jenny Nash, Head of the Education Solutions Design Team at LEGO Education, said, "A baker uses chemistry; in the blockbuster movies we see in theatres, a computer animator creates the on-screen special effects, and a chemist creates the makeup." Experiencing S.T.E.A.M. (can also be written as STEAM) subjects as a whole is more authentic and reflective of the world the next generation will be entering.

It is necessary to remember that all of the details presented above pertain to the United States of America.

Before going forward, let us explore S.T.E.M more.

S.T.E.M stands for Science, Technology, Engineering, and Mathematics. But S.T.E.M or STEM is more than just subject names. It is a philosophy of education that embraces teaching skills and subjects in a way that relates to real life and helps students solve real-world problems.

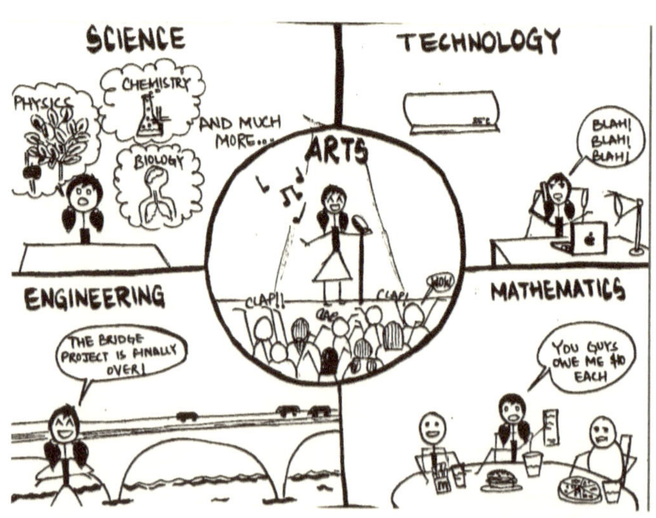

S.T.E.M. is an integration. It is about teaching to solve real-world problems via interdisciplinary learning of Science, Technology, Engineering, and Mathematics. S.T.E.M. is a curriculum a nation adopts for its students in schools and colleges.

Science, in general, includes Physics, Chemistry, Biology, and subjects of formal Science, which include Mathematics. Mathematics can cover Computer Science, Artificial Intelligence, Game Theory, etc. All countries are trying to adapt the curriculum to increase creativity, critical thinking, and practical problem-solving among students to create more innovative products and businesses within the country, to increase the GDP of the nation, and to create more job opportunities.

According to Arvind Gupta, Director of Vivekananda International Foundation, Technology and Engineering have long been a part of India's culture and civilisation. They are now playing an increasingly important role in shaping the country's future in a globalised world. The current rate of technological change in the world is unparalleled, opening up new avenues for production, knowledge development, and innovation. For India's vast population, this opens up enormous opportunities for economic development and social benefits. However, India must build and expand human expertise in the interrelated fields of Science,

Technology, Engineering, and Mathematics in order to reap these benefits.

It is critical to build people's skills so that they can be meaningfully employed in specialised STEM sectors for India's vast population, which is on the verge of rapid socio-economic transformation. STEM has an influence on nearly all forms of jobs and professions, as well as culture as a whole. As a result, it is critical that every member of society gains a thorough understanding of STEM and actively participates in it. Aside from creating jobs, potential developments in Science and technology will be critical in combating the most challenging social and environmental problems we face, and appropriately trained experts will be needed to address these issues.

The experts make many important recommendations, including the need to begin integrated B. Tech programmes that would not only encourage students' innovation and creativity but also meet the needs of India's growing small-scale industrial sector. The experts recognise the importance of instilling a scientific mindset in order to transform Indian society's strength of "Jugaad culture" into a "Culture of Innovation."

Prof. KK Agarwal, Chairman of the STEM task force, stated that today's academic institutions in India are more concerned with publications than with actual products. As a result, national missions like "Make in

India" don't get the full benefit of the country's scientists and academicians' intrinsic Research and Development (R&D) capacity. Consequently, the STEM higher education system is not being pushed to make major improvements quickly enough. It could be too late to correct the situation unless immediate action is taken. Although the rapid growth of India's service sector is welcome, it should not lead to complacency in the manufacturing sector or deter us from contributing our fair share of creativity and innovation. India is a country brimming with talent, capable of rising to any challenge, and our internal demand for high-quality goods can be very high. These factors should be sufficient to stimulate design R&D and the production of high-quality, energy-efficient, environmentally friendly, cost-effective, and long-lasting goods. It has not occurred, and we stress the importance of not wasting any more time.

STEM differs from our traditional educational streams in that it does not promote teaching and learning through textbooks or measuring learner skills through a marks-based evaluation framework. It is a contemporary approach that promotes the use of creative curricula that discourages rote learning and instead engages students in the learning process through creativity and real-world applications.

As a result, by introducing students to STEM and providing opportunities for them to investigate

STEM-related topics, they can develop an interest in the subject and, ideally, pursue a career in the area. Students can learn more by participating in a STEM-based curriculum that is enriched with real-life scenarios. Hands-on and mind-on learning are emphasised in STEM practices. In order to build a base of scientists, engineers, and the next generation of innovators, Science teachers must be educated and passionate, with the necessary skills and expertise to educate, instigate, and encourage students.

The demand for Science educators, on the other hand, continues to outstrip availability greatly. In India, there is a major STEM gap that must be bridged by teacher capacity building and high-quality educational services. Students should be better prepared to think critically and creatively. As a result of this, they will be able to become innovators, educators, scholars, and leaders. Today, some academics see these fields as launching pads for their careers. Closing this distance and cultivating a vital spirit of scientific temper and creativity is critical. [1].

There is a lot of information available on the internet that tells the importance of STEM in the Indian education system, especially at the undergraduate-level, where still rote learning is promoted in most of the institutes. But with the outbreak of diseases like Covid-19 in the world, the education pattern is shifting to the digital platform. Due to this, the students are not receiving the mentorship needed to build innovative projects associated with their area of study. So now, it is even more important for all of us to get united and step forward to create awareness about STEM.

Every parent, teacher, and student must understand the concept of STEM because this is the only way we can create a better future for our nation.

According to the National Education Policy 2020 (NEP 2020), there are various problems currently faced by the higher education system that involve undergraduate-level and graduate-level studies.

Some of the major problems currently faced by the higher education system in India include:

a. A highly fragmented higher education ecosystem.

b. A lower priority placed on the growth of cognitive skills and learning outcomes.

c. A strict division of disciplines, with early specialisation and students being funnelled into narrow fields of study.

d. Restricted access, particularly in socioeconomically disadvantaged areas.

e. Restricted autonomy for teachers and institutions.

f. Insufficient mechanisms for merit-based career management and advancement of faculty and institutional leaders.

g. Less focus on the study at most universities and schools, as well as a shortage of competitive peer-reviewed research support across disciplines.

h. Insufficient mechanisms for merit-based career management and progression of faculty and institutional leaders.

i. Wide affiliating universities result in poor undergraduate education standards.

NEP 2020 seeks to address these issues by expanding multidisciplinary courses for students that include artistic, creative, and analytical subjects as well as sports. India must restore this great Indian legacy in order to produce well-rounded and creative individuals, which is already changing other countries' educational and economic systems.

According to NEP 2020, assessments of undergraduate educational approaches that combine the humanities and Arts with Science, Technology, Engineering, and Mathematics (STEM) have consistently demonstrated positive learning outcomes, including increased interest in subjects and enjoyment of learning, enhanced imagination and innovation, critical thinking and higher-order thinking capabilities, problem-solving abilities, teamwork, communication skills, more in-depth learning and mastery of curricula across disciplines, improvements in social and moral knowledge, etc.

A comprehensive and multidisciplinary education strategy also improves and enhances research. A holistic and multidisciplinary education will strive to incorporate the development of all human capacities, including intellectual, aesthetic, social, physical, emotional, and moral values. The Arts, Humanities, Languages, Sciences, Social Sciences, and professional, technological, and vocational fields will all benefit from such an education.

A holistic and multidisciplinary education, as beautifully defined in India's past, is indeed needed for India's education to lead the country into the twenty-first century and the fourth industrial revolution. Also, Engineering schools like IITs will move to a more comprehensive, multidisciplinary curriculum that includes more arts and humanities. Students in the arts and Sciences will strive to study more Science, and all students will attempt to have more vocational subjects and soft skills. Curricular systems that are imaginative and versatile would allow for innovative combinations of disciplines to be studied, as well as many entry and exit points, eliminating the existing rigid boundaries and opening up new possibilities for lifelong learning. Graduate-level, master's, and doctoral education in broad multidisciplinary universities will offer opportunities for multidisciplinary work in academia, government, and industry, while also offering rigorous research-based specialisation.

The idea presented by NEP 2020 is clear and bold. Its vision is to promote multidisciplinary learning in all kinds of institutions in India. And its focus is on Arts, such as music, dance, theatre, dramatics, etc., because it is well established by scientists and researchers of the world that all art forms such as dramatics enhance creativity, cognitive abilities, speaking skills, teamwork spirit, leadership skills, concentration, people skills, etc., which are the top-notch skills needed in 21st-century India to create innovative strategies and products for India.

The mission of Make in India can only be achieved if manufacturing from small-scale industries is promoted with more creative products and services for the customers and other business companies. We will be looking in the chapters of this book at how dramatics play an important role in helping an individual become creative and a great problem solver for 21st-century India.

STEM curriculum is the backbone of any nation. Every country is taking steps to improve its quality of education, and all the countries aim at targeting the students. China launched a vision with STEM to become an innovative country by 2030 and an innovative power by 2050. All the countries are creating awareness among the students to take Science, technology, and Arts as their lifelong learning.

In India as well, the government took the initiative to promote STEM in 2006 by introducing Robotics labs in various schools. But the whole revolution was not much appreciated, and the results were not satisfying as robotics labs were only set up in around 3% of the total schools till 2020. One of the reasons behind its failure is that setting up a robotics lab in schools requires a lot of investment. That investment can be related to providing a robotics kit. Not many schools, especially in small towns, can convince the students or parents to make this kind of investment.

India is a market of various digital applications because building a software application does not require much investment; also, with high computerised software, such as CAD, designing hardware is also easy. This can aid students to build good hardware products for India.

An Indian show on History TV 18, "Yeh Mera India," is hosted by one of the finest comedians in India, Krushna. In the TV show, the host shares various stories related to the inventions happening in India. Once a story about Ant Studio, a design studio in Delhi, was shared. They are using the old technology of mud pots to create out-of-the-box cooling technologies for India.

Similarly, there are various problems pertaining in India, which can be solved via making some technologies by integrating the study of Physics, Chemistry, Engineering, and Arts. Arts here plays a crucial role, as practising Arts enhances one's ability to think creatively. Ant Studio is the perfect example of Arts integrated with Science and technology.

Another Pune-based startup, Kalyani Studio, is combining arts, creativity, design, and Engineering to offer brilliant solutions for the automotive industry.

Not only in technology, but MBA graduates with Arts as their passionate hobbies are also more productive and provide creative solutions to various complex problems, according to the article "4 reasons business students should study Arts" by Elizabeth Koprowski. The business professionals following Arts are leaders in the corporate world. It has been found that artists in business are creative, innovative, more relaxed, and good team leaders.

In India, STEM is not yet established properly, while other nations are working on a STEAM strategy to improve education. First, India has to transform from being a nation promoting rote learning to a nation promoting STEM learning, then to a nation working on a STEAM strategy. Instead, India should work on adopting STEAM learning directly as the way to develop a better education system. STEM and STEAM share the same goal: to boost creativity and foster innovation in a variety of fields, including medicine, defence, travel, entertainment, furniture, and food. But in a country like India, the concept of STEAM will serve better because Arts will help students to shift from rote learning habits to creative habits first, and that will ultimately help in better cognitive abilities, social skills, teamwork skills, etc., and then introduce the students to subjects of Science and technology.

Introducing Arts as a subject in Engineering colleges will also serve the purpose, as students will develop the artistic and creative approach in learning other subjects. But Arts as a subject will not suffice the purpose of building creative thinking in students; it needs a practical approach in creating experimental thinking in students. Students must be encouraged to show their creativity in various events in colleges. Participation in clubs such as dramatics, music, poetry at the college level must be encouraged, and students must understand how to mix their scientific knowledge with Arts to come up with a more innovative approach to real-world problems.

The coming chapters in the book talk about various soft skills that are necessary in the 21st century for any job or business. The chapters comprise the scientific proof about the skills that dramatics, music, or any other art form helps to develop in an individual. The chapters also build up the relationship between Science, technology, Engineering, Mathematics, business, and Arts.

Reading the chapters, you will get an understanding of how practising Arts can help students improve their grades and increase their cognitive ability, their lateral thinking, and building leadership skills. The chapters are designed to assist people in comprehending the broad relationship between their many fields and the Arts, as well as how they might combine their technical, scientific, and business expertise with the Arts.

In the next 50 years, the STEAM system of education must be established for a better future for India. STEAM can only revolutionise the prime minister's vision of "Atmanirbhar Bharat."

Establishing a dramatics club in every Engineering or Science college is important; similarly, establishing a Technological club in every Arts college is also very important to promote the vision of STEAM.

I can vividly explain the importance of Dramatics in Engineering colleges because that was the only way that helped me understand the importance of creativity, critical thinking, and teamwork for the 21st century. Dramatics taught me various soft skills and helped me understand the importance of those skills when I started writing this book. Now let us move to the next chapter, which explains the importance of the "Dramatics club" in every Engineering and MBA college.

Dramatics

"Tell me, and I will forget. Show me, and I will remember. Involve me, and I will understand."

The proverb mentioned above by Benjamin Franklin is the soul of any learning. If you want to learn anything, you must get yourself involved in the process. You have to practically experiment with the procedure to get an understanding of the whole process.

The current Indian educational system is mostly centered on rote learning, or learning by reading and practicing; this increases the amount of time students spend studying because they must repeat topics numerous times in order to retain them in their minds. This is how we train our brains. Rote learning has its importance. It makes you habitual with the theories and gives you a chance to apply that rote learning without opening the book multiple times.

The study of Science is more about experimentation, and Engineering is about applying those experiments to create technology. When we talk about management, it is about experimenting with new strategies multiple times to gain experience and knowledge and then applying that knowledge to complete a task efficiently and at the optimum time.

Experimentation is a very important skill needed to create a unique idea, strategy, or product. Experimenting is a result of curiosity, and experiments are needed in every field that you work in, be it website designing, sales execution, content creation, writing, technical research, marketing, or even setting up a business from scratch.

In India, students are so well-planned with their careers, due to influence from their peers or elders, that they do not even experiment or build up their experimental temperament. We will see how dramatics can act as a stimulus in developing this mindset.

Dramatics can be defined as the study or practice of acting and producing plays. Drama can have many forms, like acting on a stage, Mime, which is storytelling with the help of gestures with background music or a poem. There can be a radio drama as well, which is just storytelling with voice modulation and tone changing.

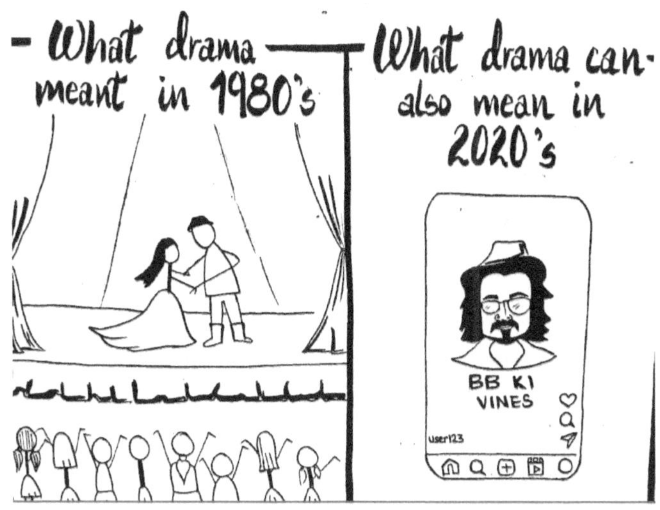

Nowadays, the definition of drama is also changing, with the evolution of YouTube and Instagram. Now, various art forms are growing, such as band music, electronic music, hip-hop, and even rapping; there can be various new experiments that can be done, like acting on raps or Mime on hip-hop music. This all sounds strange, but it justifies the definition of dramatics. The main aim of dramatics is to convey the right thought in a way that others find it attractive.

The American Association of School Administrators, The Alliance for Education, and The John F. Kennedy Center for the Performing Arts published Performing Together: The Arts and Education in 1985. It clearly tells that Dramatic Arts education is an important tool for encouraging problem-solving and innovation. It has the potential to question students' views of the world and of themselves. Dramatic exploration will give students a way to convey feelings, ideas, and dreams that they may not be able to express otherwise. If only for a few moments, a student can take on another person's identity, explore a new role, try out and experiment with different personal choices and solutions to very real problems—problems from their own lives or problems faced by characters in history.

This can be done in a controlled environment, where behaviour and effects can be studied, addressed, and learned without the risks and drawbacks that such experimentation would bring in the actual world. The importance of Dramatic Arts in schools is perhaps the most significant reason. Even then, drama has a lot more to offer.

Communication is at the heart of all drama. Drama, like all of the Arts, helps students to interact with and appreciate others in new ways. Drama, maybe more than any other art form, teaches the very practical aspects of communication that are so important in today's increasingly information-centric world. Students who engage in dramatic events are less likely to have public speaking difficulties, are more convincing in their written and oral interactions, and are better able to put themselves in others' shoes and relate to them. They have a more optimistic and encouraging self-image.

Dramatic behaviour generally requires self-control and discipline, which will benefit the student in all facets of life. Drama students can learn to collaborate, find the best way for each member of a community to participate, and listen to and consider the opinions and contributions of others. There is no other art form that is genuinely collaborative. Drama is a valuable tool for preparing students to live and work in a world that is becoming more team-oriented rather than hierarchical.

The drama also promotes tolerance and empathy among students. An actor must be able to fully inhabit another's soul in order to play a role well. An actor must be able to see the world through the eyes of another person. This does not imply that he has to agree with all of the characters. It is possible for an actor to play Hitler without becoming a Nazi. But he can't play Hitler unless he understands and empathises with his point of view. Understanding others' motives and choices is critical in today's increasingly polarised and intolerant culture. Drama can assist in the development of responsible global citizens. Drama, in addition to its inherent educational value, can be used to supplement the rest of the school curriculum. Because drama emphasises communication and empathy, a student who has explored like in the drama classroom will have a better understanding of historical and current events. He will be able to put himself in the shoes of historical and literary figures, comprehend how people interact, and see the connection between dramatic Arts and subjects like **English, history, social studies, and even Science**. Without drama, studying literature would be impossible. During certain periods in our collective literary history, nearly all of the surviving literature is dramatic. Drama, moreover, can be used to promote active learning in any subject by providing students with a kinesthetic, empathetic, and intellectual understanding of a topic. Studies have repeatedly shown that this approach leads to a greater depth of understanding and a significant increase in retention. [2].

Overall, dramatics gives us a chance to experiment with different things such as expressions, screenplay, scripts, acting, etc. It also helps us understand various social problems emphatically. It helps in developing a creative mindset, cognitive ability, good concentration, people skills, social skills, and leadership qualities. We will be looking at these topics one by one in the book, and we will also understand their importance in the 21st century. We will be looking at how Dramatics can help in fulfilling the vision of STEAM, especially in India.

The most important skill that dramatics helps in developing is creativity, which is an outcome of experiments. Let us begin the next chapter of the book. "CREATIVITY'.

Creativity

Creativity! The first thing that hit my mind about creativity is the book *Creativity, Inc.* that is written by Ed Catmull, the book with an image of Buzz Lightyear, a character from the movie Toy Story. It is one of the finest books available to learn the actual definition of creativity in the field of Science, technology, and business. It is the story of Pixar, one of the finest animation studios on this planet. Creativity has always been a crucial part of humanity, and we are using creativity every day, without even knowing about it. Creativity can be defined as the use of imagination or original ideas to create something unique; this book itself is an example of creativity.

Creativity is necessary for every field in this 21st-century era of technology where every day something new is created. In the field of animation, creativity is necessary to create unique art for entertainment. In the music industry, creativity is required to create the most soothing lyrics fitting over heart-touching beats. In dramatics, creativity is required to create the most astonishing scene on camera or stage. In the field of sports, creativity is necessary to put a unique strategy on the field.

Similarly, in the field of Science and technology, this creativity is necessary to promote new inventions which are necessary to create new businesses and to create more jobs for people, especially in a country like India. The Indian government has always taken important steps to encourage kids to be creative. One of the major steps was promoting STEM. Many schools are adopting this curriculum worldwide. The curriculum was started to educate students about various Science and technological fields, where they

Can create something new and help the nation grow, but the curriculum is incomplete because to come up with unique inventions, "creativity and innovation" are of utmost importance. Due to this reason, one more subject, Arts, was added to the curriculum and STEM was converted to STEAM where 'A' stands for Arts. There are still many researches going on to integrate Arts with STEM worldwide, but in India, people are not much aware of it. The importance of creativity cannot be overstated. The word "creative" conjures up images of novelists, poets, composers, and visual artists in the minds of many ordinary people. They would acknowledge the creativity of Mathematicians/physicists like Einstein or inventors like Thomas Edison if prompted, but there is a general tendency to associate creativity with the Arts rather than the Sciences. In fact, Arts and creativity are inextricably linked. Without a doubt, the Arts have given people all over the world the opportunity to find solutions to long-standing problems. Science, on the other hand, is linked to creativity. The author, Alexandra Ossola, claims in her article "Scientists Are More Creative Than You Might Imagine" that scientists are just as creative as the artists in question. Arts and Science, on the other hand, are undeniably connected to innovation. [3]

Every great innovator, including Da Vinci, Einstein, Steve Jobs, and Elon Musk, was also a superb artist. Art in itself is a vast field which can include acting, poetry, creative writing, storytelling, rapping, video editing, music production, painting, dancing, etc., and every subject has its importance as every subject helps in learning different kinds of soft skills, but more or less, every subject helps in developing creative thinking. Inventors always have tried to train the left and right brains together to come up with better inventions. Similarly, many engineers have adopted this strategy to come up with unique solutions to different problems. If a mechanical engineer is unable to invent something on the mechanical front, he is of no use. In most Indian institutes, many resources such as labs, availability of mentors with scientific temperament, newest software, and their knowledge are not available. As a result, finding resources to use for their objectives becomes harder for them. Students in colleges should become involved in a variety of clubs that will help them develop their creativity. Creativity is one of the most important soft skills, which help people, not only of scientific background but also help people involved in managerial roles. Creativity cannot be improved just by reading theories. It can only be enhanced by experimenting and trying new things in real life. Dramatics is an exercise that students can do to improve their creativity.

Drama allows people to experiment with their personalities, writing, screenplays, and other aspects of their lives. Experiments with Drama, like scientific experiments, can fail at times, but if they succeed, they can produce magnificent goods, such as plays or music, that people would adore. The same can be said about scientific research; if the tests work, the impact on humanity will be enormous. There is a relationship between dramatics and Science, that both involve experimentation as the best means to create something new. As a result, practising drama can undoubtedly assist people in developing experimental skills that will aid them in scientific experiments, which are far more dangerous. Experiments are also linked to creativity. Creativity has always helped people in all domains to come up with unique solutions. After the extensive practice of experimenting new on the field, creativity can be developed in the best way, as it will push you to make mistakes multiple times and every time learning from previous mistakes, you come up with better solutions. Arts play a very important role in developing creativity as it gives you a chance to experiment multiple times without any kind of investment. Nowadays, many people are taking YouTube as their career.

People are trying to use their creativity to come up with good entertaining series, knowledge-based creations, or even great movies, and this cannot be achieved without a good creative thinking mindset. People are motivated by the Arts to be more creative and, as a result, to improve in a variety of ways. Consider the programme "Learning through the Arts" (Upitis and Smithrim, 2005). This approach was developed by the Royal Conservatory of Music in Canada. Essentially, this programme looked into the impact of the Arts on schooling. The LTTA programme compared and measured student results between schools that participated in the programme and those that did not. Students in the LTTA programme, as expected, received higher grades than those in the other programmes after three years. As a result, kids showed remarkable progress.

This is also emphasised in the film "The Finland Phenomenon." Finland's educational system is very different from that of other countries. The methods used in these schools are unique, from teachers to classrooms. Arts, on the other hand, have a significant presence in Finland. Essentially, Arts are given in a variety of methods to these children. Painting, music, and the freedom to express oneself are all examples of art. It is apparent that pupils in Finland have earned better scores thus far, indicating that Arts have obviously aided kids in becoming more creative. As a result, Finland is sometimes referred to as the world's Design Capital. Arts allow for more imaginative expression. People's minds are opened when they are exposed to great art, such as music or literature. Being surrounded by art creates a template of quality and standard of excellence that can propel your creativity forward, according to Jordan Driediger's essay "7 Ways To Increase Your Creativity" (Jordan Driediger, 2007). The author then goes on to say the following: "There is nothing wrong with researching and even imitating portions of your industry's legends. Good artists copy, great artists steal," as Pablo Picasso famously said. [3] Many technological industries, be it automobiles, electronics, or even software development, follow the same philosophy of 'Stealing'.

In industries, whenever a new product is developed, a study is conducted through which the products of other industries are studied, and some kind of comparison matrices are formed to evaluate the product performance. This process is termed as 'benchmarking'. Benchmarking is just a way of stealing the methods and not the products. Creativity has its own importance in businesses as well.

In business, creativity is a method of thinking that motivates, challenges, and assists individuals in coming up with new ideas and chances to solve problems.

The most in-demand ability today, according to LinkedIn, is creative thinking. Other researchers have ranked it among the top three talents needed to run a firm (together with critical thinking and problem-solving). The visionaries who drive a company's growth and innovation activities are creative thinkers. [4]

Without creativity, a business cannot survive. In this competitive environment, a firm with a strong creative staff is constantly coming up with innovative methods to transform the way customers buy items. Creativity helps businesses to come up with unique strategies to tackle real-world problems in minimal time. Creativity in business is a subject that cannot be summarised in this small chapter, but for an example, let us consider the company 'Apple'.

Apple is an epitome of a creative business company; you can read more about it on the internet or in any of the books associated with Steve Jobs. When a 10-year-old youngster wants to make a good movie for his mother and father's wedding anniversary, for example, his inventiveness is not always recognised. Although the movie was not as creative as the kind of effects or music used by the kid were not good, but the process he used to impress his parents was worth appreciating. This can be termed as lateral thinking of the kid. Lateral thinking is a term first used by Edward de Bono in 1967 in his book "The Use of Lateral Thinking." There is a little bit of difference between being creative and having lateral thinking.

Sometimes the end product is not much appreciated, but the process used to generate the end product is full of learning. This process can be a part of lateral thinking, which is a combination of creative ideas. For example, the company Apple is an outcome of the whole lateral thinking process, with the use of creativity in its various aspects such as the logo, product, marketing strategy, sales strategy, etc. Arts give a chance to people, especially kids, to enhance their lateral thinking abilities. I am sure this thing will help them to become a creative person at some point in their life.

Concentration and Cognition

Concentration is the word that we have heard many times in our life, and everyone desires to have it as high as possible.

Whenever we discuss concentration, we also discuss meditation as the method to improve it.

But we never count on arts, music, and other extra-curricular activities. For us, these activities are just free time hobbies and nothing else. We never thought that there might be some relation between arts, typically music, and concentration. So, we will discuss how art helps in improving concentration, how it is indirect meditation, and what is the connection between concentration and Arts as indirect meditation?

Before we go further, let us understand what concentration is. Concentration is defined as the action or power of focusing one's attention.

That seems so easy. We have to focus on one single thought and avoid other thoughts that are randomly coming into our mind. But wait, do you realise how many random thoughts pass through our heads every day? There are different answers to this question like 60,000, 70,000, 6,000, etc. Let us consider 6,000 for an example. So, if 6,000 thoughts are coming into our mind daily, it will result in 250 thoughts per hour, which means if we are told to concentrate on a particular thing for an hour, then we must make sure that these random thoughts are not influencing us. We can understand by this example that it seems easy until we start focusing on something. As we start focusing on some thought, we go with the thought initially, but after a few seconds, we are lost in the pool of some other random thoughts. So, focusing on a single thought out of 250 for an hour is as easy as selecting a single cloth from the cluster of 250 clothes, and do not forget that all the 250 clothes are eye-catching.

Now the question arises: how can we improve our concentration or focus?

And most of the time the answer to this question is meditation, and it is the tested way to improve it. Now another question that comes to mind is, what is meditation?

Meditation is a method of training attention and awareness, as well as achieving a cognitively clear, emotionally peaceful, and stable state, via the application of a technique such as mindfulness or focusing the mind on a specific object, thought, or activity. It implies that we must concentrate on a single object and maintain consistency in our efforts.

For sure, we can have good focus if we practice meditation regularly, but to practice it, we must be mature enough to understand it. What about the children and teenage people who don't have a deep understanding of it? They have the leverage of their active mind that can quickly do things as compared to older people. What if some more focus could be added to their minds most creatively? What if they could have some indirect kind of meditation?

Is meditation the only way to improve focus? Some people might say yes to this question, but I can't entirely agree with this.

There are many other ways that can improve focus. Did you know that music, dance, poetry, drama, and many other such kinds of activities help a lot in improving it? Unfortunately, they are extra-curricular activities. However, in the upcoming days, they will not be extra-curricular because they will be part of the curriculum. So, it is a good time to understand it more. Let us discuss how focus improves by practising any form of art.

Take the example of a piano. If someone starts learning piano, then at first, he must train his hands. Our hands are trained to do the symmetric work, but while playing the piano, the case is different. On the one hand, we have to play the chords, and on the other, we have to play the notes. So, the motion of each hand is different, and it needs practice and focus both; that is why it is a kind of indirect meditation. Because most of the time, the mind is focused on a single thing. Many studies show that a person has a much higher focus if he plays any musical instrument as compared to others who are not involved in any such kind of activities.

In fact, rapping also helps in increasing concentration because it involves a long time speaking words fluently on the correct beat. An article in Data Foundation discusses the value of art in boosting attention and cognition, as well as how it can benefit other disciplines like Math and Science when done on a daily basis.

Let us try to understand the term cognition as well.

The mental processes involved in learning knowledge and comprehension are referred to as cognition. Thinking, knowing, remembering, judging, and problem-solving are examples of cognitive processes. Language, imagination, perception, and planning are examples of higher-level brain activities. [5]

In short, Cognition can be defined as the process of understanding things and gaining knowledge.

Now let us try to understand the article in Data Foundation about the importance of Arts in improving attention and cognition.

Would you try it if there was a surefire way to boost your brain? Many individuals are lining up for quick brain fixes, judging by the profusion of products, programmes, and medications that claim to deliver "cognitive enhancement."

A recent study suggests that focused training in any of the Arts, such as music, dance, or theatre, develops the brain's attention system, which can boost cognition more broadly. Furthermore, this strengthening most likely explains the effects of Arts training on the brain and cognitive performance that have been described in a number of scientific research, including those presented in May 2009 at a Johns Hopkins University neuroeducation summit. The brain has a system of neuronal circuits dedicated to attention, as we know. We already know that training these attention networks enhances general IQ measurements. And we can be quite certain that focusing our attention on learning and performing art activates these similar attention networks if we practice frequently and are sincerely interested. As a result, we can expect targeted Arts instruction to increase cognition in general.

This argument may appear to be a bold association jump to some, yet it is based on solid Science. The attention system is the lynchpin in this equation. The importance of attention in cognitive performance is undeniable since it plays a critical role in learning and memory. Pay attention if you want to learn something! This is something we all intuitively understand, and there is plenty of scientific evidence to back it up.

In the context of what we call activity-dependent plasticity, a basic premise of brain function, the claim that Arts instruction improves cognition, in general, isn't that audacious. It indicates that your brain changes as a result of your actions. To put it another way, behaviour shapes and sculpts brain networks in the following way: What you do in your day-to-day life is reflected in the wiring patterns of your brain and the efficiency of your brain's networks. Perhaps nowhere is this more evident than in your attention networks.

Most of us should notice gains in other cognitive areas where attention is key, such as learning and memory, as well as increasing cognition in general if we find something that "works" for us—that incites our enthusiasm and engages us wholeheartedly—and continue with it.

If our hypothesis is correct, why have scientists been unable to establish a cause-and-effect relationship between Arts education and cognition, such as "[X] amount of training in art form [Y] results in a [Z] per cent increase in IQ scores"? Because there are so many variables at play, such a relationship is difficult to demonstrate experimentally; scientists have only just begun to look at this relationship in a systematic, rigorous manner.

The so-called **"Mozart Effect"** was the focus of early research into the theory that the Arts might improve brainpower. According to the letter published in the journal Nature in 1993, college students who were exposed to classical music enhanced their spatial thinking skills, which are critical for academic achievement in Math and Science. This insight sparked a marketing frenzy that has lasted to this day. Despite several attempts, scientists have not been able to duplicate the event reliably. Nonetheless, rather than formal musical training or practice, these investigations comprised brief periods of exposure to music.

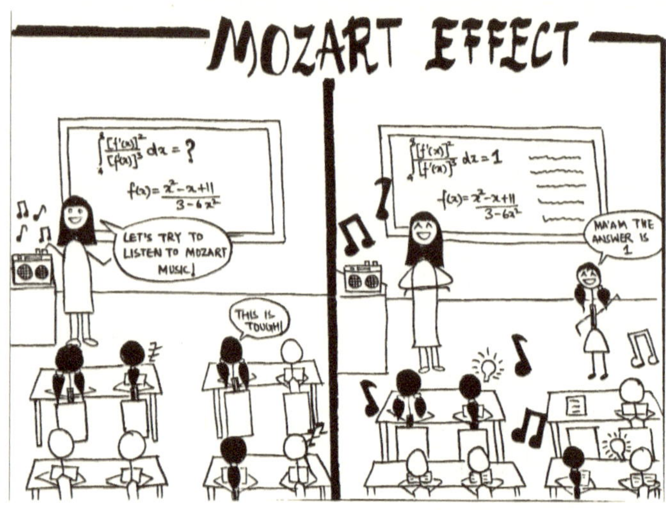

A distinct method has been used in recent attempts to link Arts instruction with general advances in cognition. Rather than being exposed to music, researchers have focused on extended durations of involved engagement and practice in Arts training. For example, in 2004, E. Glenn Schellenberg of the University of Toronto at Mississauga published results from a randomised trial. The IQ scores of 72 children involved in a yearlong music training programme increased significantly when compared to 36 children who received no training and 36 children who attended theatre lessons, according to a controlled study. (While the IQ scores of children who took drama training did not improve, they did improve more than the other groups in terms of judgements of specific social skills.)

Researchers Ellen Winner of Boston College, Gottfried Schlaug of Harvard University, and their colleagues at McGill University used neuroimaging scans to assess brain changes in young children who undertook a four-year music training programme, according to a study published in the Journal of NeuroScience in March 2009—compared to a control group of kids who didn't get any music lessons. The researchers discovered structural alterations in brain regions involved in music processing in the children who received training in the first round of testing, which took place after 15 months. The control group did not show the same changes.

The researchers also discovered that musically relevant motor and auditory abilities improved, a process known as a close transfer.

Studying an issue or task and then practising it to a high level of automaticity is known as a near-transfer. When an issue or task that is almost identical is encountered, it is solved or completed automatically with little or no conscious thought.

Take, for instance, tying shoelaces. When we learn to tie a shoelace, it's very likely that we'll be able to tie any shoelace, regardless of length, colour, or thickness of the lace or the shoe's design.

Studying an issue or task and then practising it to a high level of automaticity is known as a near-transfer. [6]

The evidence suggests that music training can alter brain circuitry and, in some cases, improve general cognition.

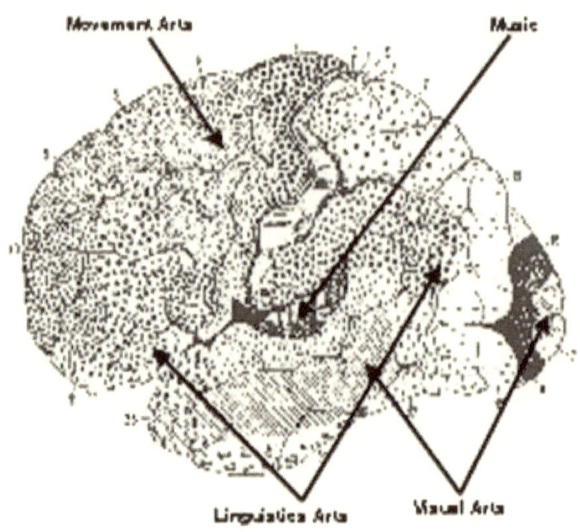

Practising a skill, whether in the Arts or in other fields, generates a broad repertoire of relevant material. Scientists studying numerous human tasks with neuroimaging have discovered networks of widely dispersed brain regions that work together to complete a task, which may include sensory, motor, attentional, affective, and language functions. The Arts are no different: As seen in Figure 1, specific brain networks underpin particular art forms. As we practise a task, its underlying network becomes more efficient, and connections among brain areas that perform different aspects of the task become more tightly integrated.

This is similar to an orchestra performing a symphony. The music created by combining orchestral pieces is likely to sound more fluent the hundredth time they perform it than the first.

Repeated activation of the brain's attention networks boosts their efficiency, according to a significant body of scientific research. Various components of attention are also underpinned by the following specific brain networks, according to neuroimaging research. **Executive attention skills, especially the abilities to control emotions and to focus thoughts (sometimes called cognitive control), are critical aspects of social and academic success throughout childhood.** Empathy for others, the ability to manage reward-motivated impulses, and even the ability to manage the proclivity to cheat or lie have all been linked to executive attention in scientific studies. Researchers have also discovered that measurements of the network's efficiency are linked to student achievement. [6]

Given the importance of the executive attention network, it's crucial to figure out what it's all about. To explore the impact of attention-training exercises in 4 to 6-year-old children, researchers used a set of exercises originally meant to train monkeys for space travel. The youngsters were randomly assigned to either a control condition (which comprised watching and responding to interactive movies) or training on joystick-operated computer exercises that were designed to activate attention networks through motivation and reward (see the image at the top right). They inserted noninvasive electrodes on the children's scalps to look at their brain activity after they completed five days of computer exercises for around 30 minutes per day; they found signs of enhanced efficiency in the executive attention network. In contrast to the control groups, the experimental group's network performance approximated that of adults. This improved performance was reflected in higher results on IQ testing for young children. [6]

These findings show that improving the executive attention network's efficiency also improves general cognition as assessed by IQ. M. Rosario Rueda and colleagues from the University of Granada in Spain later replicated this critical finding in an unpublished study of Spanish children. Attention-training, according to Rueda, improved the children's ability to delay gratification, and the improvements persisted for at least two months after training. [6]

Many children's enthusiasm for a particular art form translates into sustained attention when that art form is practiced. Furthermore, participating in art frequently necessitates resolving conflicts among competing viable answers, such as when selecting the appropriate note to play at a certain time. A fundamental part of attention-training is the ability to resolve conflict among conflicting reactions. If you're supposed to reply to a target arrow by hitting a key in the direction the arrowhead points, adding surrounding arrows pointing in the opposite direction will speed up your reaction time and activate elements of the executive attention network. As a result, we anticipate that Arts instruction will strengthen the executive attention network and, therefore, improve cognition in general. [6]

With breakthroughs in neuroscience giving crucial new tools for studying cognition, researchers and educators must collaborate to plan and implement studies that build on the findings that Arts training has near-transfer effects and discover whether this training also has far-transfer cognitive benefits. [6]

Let's get a better understanding of the concept of long-distance transfer. Consider a situation where every door has a lever handle or a knob to turn, and you come across one that has neither. Instead, it has a push-button next to the door on the wall. [6]

So, what exactly do you do? We must learn to broaden our skillset to embrace a larger range of situations, as well as develop higher-level mental models that will allow us to tackle challenges that are even more difficult to handle than the ones we initially encountered. Rather than directly applicable automated methods, we are now conveying principles that influence problem-solving. This is referred to as distant transfer. Far-transfer tasks entail the application of skills and knowledge in contexts that change, with the skill application differing depending on the scenario. In far-transfer, the learner modifies their behaviours according to their judgement in any situation. [6]

As we've seen, contemporary research has moved beyond the flawed paradigm of simply introducing people to the arts and now focuses on the long-term consequences of arts instruction. More research like this is needed to discover whether there is causation beyond strong association. Other brain mechanisms may also alter cognition as a result of Arts instruction. Because arts training increases the brain network relevant to the art being practiced, other tasks that rely on the same or portions of the same brain circuitry are likely to be impacted.

We could expect to see improvements in non-musical tasks involving pitch if music training influences the auditory system. Indeed, Brian Wandell and his Stanford University colleagues have established that youngsters who participate in music or the visual arts have better phonological awareness or the capacity to alter speech sounds, which is linked to reading fluency. Moreover, the more music training they had, the better their reading fluency.

Also, elements of the music network are close to sections of the brain involved in number processing, which could explain anecdotal accounts of arithmetic benefits following music instruction. For example, Harvard University's Elizabeth Spelke discovered that school-aged youngsters who received intense music training performed better on abstract geometry exercises. Wandell and his colleagues also presented preliminary findings linking visual Arts experience with children's Math calculation abilities. Future research will need to go deeper into these possibilities.

Another fascinating facet of the Performing Arts is that artists frequently prepare for their performances by purposefully entering a state of mind that they believe would improve their performance, such as deep breathing, visualizing the moment, or other meditation practices. Yi-Yuan Tang, a visiting professor at the University of Oregon from Dalian Medical University in China, recently reported that some forms of meditation could produce changes in the connection between the brain and the parasympathetic branch of the autonomic nervous system and, after just a few days of training, can lead to improvements in the same aspects of executive attention that are trained by specifically exercising this network. This "attention state" also correlates with improved mood and resistance to stress.

The expanding body of empirical evidence suggests that Arts instruction might improve cognitive function—including our hypothesis, which identifies better attention networks as the mechanism—opens up a new field of research for cognitive scientists. The latest research findings provide yet another reason for parents and educators to encourage young people to select an art form they enjoy and follow with zeal. Continuing study in this area might also explain ongoing arguments regarding the value of Arts education, which has crucial policy implications in light of budgetary pressures to eliminate Arts programmes from the school curriculum.

From our perspective, it is becoming increasingly obvious that Arts instruction, when combined with enough concentrated attention, can produce cognitive benefits that go beyond "art for the sake of art." To put it another way, learning an art form that you truly enjoy may lead to advances in other aspects of your brain.

All of the data shown above was gathered from a variety of sources in order to show the benefits of Arts in increasing a person's concentration and cognitive abilities.

Suppose you've ever studied or practiced an art form in school or college, attempt to gain a better grasp of it and put it to use further. It will not only offer you a distinct identity, but it will also strengthen your brain networks. Practising any art form can undoubtedly assist you in any of your daily tasks, whether it is driving a car or giving a 5-minute presentation. People who are interested in a particular art form frequently prefer to preserve it as a pastime rather than commit enough time to it in order to polish it or excel at it. As a result, they didn't perceive any improvements in their other responsibilities.

But as mentioned in the chapter, passionately following the art form can give you immense power to have good control over your brain, to carry out another task easily and in minimum time. Integrating the Arts with Science and technology is beneficial because practising the arts improves brain networks that, in general, increase the cognitive ability to grasp Science concepts and the logical ability to apply Mathematics concepts to solve real-world problems by intensely focusing on the problem and avoiding random thoughts in the shortest amount of time.

Yes, it is truly said that art is a form of indirect meditation.

Team Work and Leadership

In this chapter, we will talk about Teamwork and leadership and their role in accomplishing a mission and how arts provide opportunities to work in teams and help learn new things.

A team comprises people with different mindsets, feelings, attitudes, styles, behavior, skills, and talent. It is always challenging for a leader to guide other people in the same direction to make a dream come true. If we look into the organizations, be it school, college, a company, or a startup, they all work in teams, and there is a leader to guide them. The leader is not a superhuman being, but a leader is a person with a different mindset and skills to carry everyone forward.

Every person in a team is crucial to complete a task, and every person's input must be appreciated. Suppose that input or idea is not acceptable. In that case, the person should be criticized healthily by everyone else in the team to improve the thinking ability of that person. A team grows together. Many people in a team fight, become angry, or upset if their idea is not appreciated. This kind of behavior is not suitable for a team in completing the task, this is because most of the productive time of the team goes in solving other unproductive issues. Working in a team is a skill set that every student must learn to work efficiently in any organisation.

Have you ever thought that pursuing Arts as a subject can be a great way to develop this skill?

Here, I will be connecting some dots to explain how Dramatics can be highly beneficial and healthy in developing this skill set. I would be emphasizing more on Dramatics, as I have some personal experiences with the same. As I already mentioned, Dramatics has always been so close to me. Let me share some incidents of our dramatics team in college.

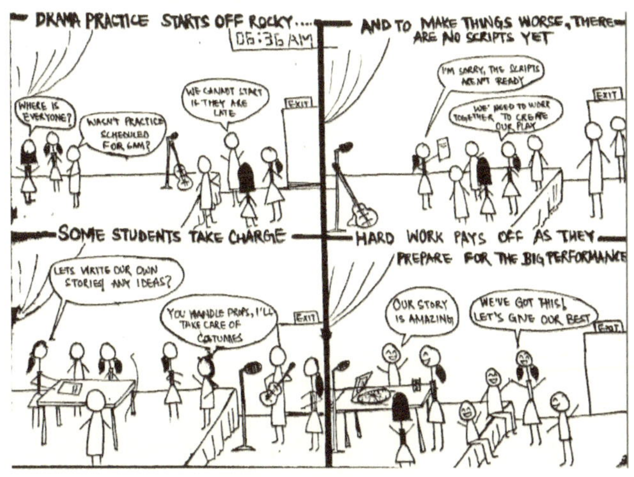

During my second-year internship, our club decided to represent our college at one of the national events associated with drama. After reading about many events on the internet, we finally decided to go for the IIM Lucknow event. It was easy for all the members to go to a nearby location from our college. My college was HBTI Kanpur, a not so famous college in Uttar Pradesh, India. The event was scheduled for five months from the date we were discussing the same. We started working on a new script that we later named "Khazane Ki Kahani." It was a script made by all of us, with a lot of experiments on characters, screenplay, costumes, etcetera. It was challenging to lead a team of 22 people to accomplish this task.

As I was the one who took the responsibility to go on stage after five months, it was probably my duty to encourage everyone to come out of their comfort zones and give it a shot. There were many problems associated with this project. First of all, it was tough to provide roles to everyone in the club. Not a single script was available online that could assign roles to everyone in the club, so as per the demand of our club, we started writing the script. There were many flaws in the play's story, but it was not a big issue as a team can make a lousy script go viral. The same is the case with startups; a great idea may not become a business. Still, a simple idea with extensive hard work of a team can turn into a business. We started working on the play without thinking much about the flaws in the script. There were also many issues associated with various members of the club. Some were very lazy to work on the script, some were unhappy with their roles, some were highly talented, and some were there to learn new things. But as the leader of the project, it was my duty to motivate everyone and use their skills in the right direction to win this competition, and we failed. We came third, which was not at all acceptable to any of us. But a team works together and fights together. We all stood up and were determined to put on our college's first-ever dramatics night, and this time we succeeded. I believe that the one who is leading a team must be open to all sorts of criticisms and must be available to learn new things from all other team members.

An article by Stacy Goodman on "7 leadership skills fostered in Arts education" clearly states that students engaged in Arts develop various skills such as creativity and a self-learning attitude, which are essential to becoming future leaders. Involvement in Arts such as poetry, acting, singing, and writing allows students to study various issues that have a profound impact on the world. For example, when I was in college, I had the opportunity to work on a play "Philosophy on Trial", where I portrayed the character of Socrates in the modern world. During that time, I learned about his personality and how his thoughts have influenced society. When we understand the perspectives and ideas of such prominent personalities, we evolve in our understanding and involuntarily develop the characteristics of these personalities.

Stacy Goodman highlighted seven skills developed by involving in activities associated with art and craft.[7]

1. Creativity

While this may appear to be the most evident skill, it is important to note that creativity encompasses more than just expression and beauty. It is also about solving problems. While other disciplines encourage creative problem-solving approaches, the Arts look for solutions that go beyond our shared knowledge of the problem, stretching the boundaries of what can be proven. Artists are the forerunners in conceiving and experimenting with new concepts and sensibilities. This is an excellent attribute for a leader.

2. Risk-Taking

If we want our students to be truly creative and seek out new ideas and viewpoints, we must encourage and reward them for taking chances. One of the most enjoyable aspects of teaching kids in the Arts is that it provides them with the capacity and confidence to try new and unconventional things. When you're an adult, peer pressure doesn't go away. When required, great leaders will go against the grain in terms of thinking and risk having their ideas and actions mocked or attacked.

Students who are typically excluded are drawn to the Arts because they have previously faced the challenge of being rejected or scorned. They've weathered the storm and are no longer afraid of being different or accepting new ideas.

3. Learning to Be Yourself

"It's lonely at the top," as the cliché goes, is one of the most difficult aspects of being a leader. Students who are nourished through the Arts must eventually look within to uncover their own potential, face their demons, and know themselves. While collaboration and teamwork are applauded, those approaches are more effective if each member of the team has gone through the solitary process of self-reflection and self-awareness.

If leaders are prepared to take chances and stand on their own, it is simpler to make a decision that may not be popular — and this is frequently the very essence of an artist (painter Vincent Van Gogh and dancer Martha Graham come to mind).

4. Understanding the Power of Myth and Symbols

Students are urged to work with icons, forms, and archetypes in art lessons so that they may grasp how these pictures influence human civilisation. Great leaders recognise how myths and symbols affect our perception of a complex notion or sensibility that is difficult to communicate otherwise.

As Martin Luther King, Jr. demonstrated, the capacity to tap into myth and iconography is always potent — and frequently lyrical and beautiful. (As Hitler demonstrated, it may also be harmful.) Artists, poets, and musicians have a keen understanding of what moves and shapes us, and student leaders should benefit from studying and mastering this.

5. Observational Skills

Great leaders are able to sense moods, attitudes, and the environment around them. We want our kids to be careful observers in Arts instruction. In addition, kids who are drawn to the Arts are frequently introverted but skilled observers. Teachers must cultivate this gift of observation in kids and help them improve it when necessary. We must also be able to recognise, cultivate, and utilise the function of the quiet influencer, which is frequently played by our most observant kids.

6. Project Planning

The most practical of the skills taught in Arts education is project planning. Students are encouraged to think about and commit to projects that are difficult to complete in weeks or months. Project planning skills generate character and tenacity in our kids who know they are in it for the long haul, in addition to applying tactics such as backward design, goal setting, and implementing an effective process.

7. Collaboration and Appropriation

While the Arts value originality above all else, we also recognise that referring to and emulating others who have mastered their skill is an essential component of the learning process. Learning from people who have gone before you can also help you learn and collaborate with people around you. Plagiarism or "copying" becomes less of a concern, and pupils learn that the line between "I" and "you" is hazy, if not imaginary. This ability to recognise oneself in others, learn and collaborate with others, is critical to understanding leadership and should be encouraged and developed in our classrooms.

All the skills mentioned by Stacy are highlighted with respect to art and craft, but if we are engaged with any activity such as drama, music, or creative

writing, we tend to develop these skills to become future leaders.[7]

Working in a team always helps a person learn new things related to culture, food, dressing sense, technology, business, money, and people because none of these mentioned topics are subjects in the Indian education curriculum.

Working in a team helps in improving communication, presentation skills, increases the confidence of an individual, promotes creativity, helps in increasing the knowledge bank of an individual, and helps in developing problem-solving skills in a quite innovative way. In this 21st-century era of technological inventions, research, and business, these skills are mandatory to succeed in any field.

Teamwork is a skill that can be developed by working in a team, and working in a team helps in learning other soft skills such as creativity and problem-solving, which are essential skills required to come up with good solutions to various problems in different fields. Students in schools and colleges must be given many projects in teams, and I believe that any kind of project related to Arts can be fun and helpful at the same time. India is seeing a paradigm shift from a competition-based nation where every individual fights for a seat in IIT, IIM, or cracks IAS to an entrepreneurial state, where new ideas are booming and creating new business opportunities for youngsters; this ultimately helps our nation grow.

Arts is one of the best means in developing many soft skills and providing opportunities to work in teams, which provides an opportunity to gain knowledge by interacting with others. People see Arts as a hobby and not as a subject. In this digital era, talented ones are also getting the chance to work and interact with other people with similar interests. This has given opportunities to various artists to earn for themselves, taking an example of Spitfire from Madhya Pradesh, who is working on his YouTube channel and Spotify for publicity and performing shows at various locations in the city to earn.

Artists should be encouraged; this will create more opportunities in the future for students with the same interests. I am not saying that every student having an interest in Arts should go for it full time; this is dependent on the student and which field he wants to explore. I am in favour of taking Arts as a subject, just like other subjects such as history, geography, or Science.

Arts as a subject is healthy and beneficial in solving real-world problems.

Gesticulation

We saw in previous chapters how theatre and other forms of art related to it can help an individual become more creative and focused. Now we'll learn about yet another soft skill: **gesticulation.**

A gesture, especially a dramatic one, used instead of speaking or to accentuate one's words, is referred to as gesticulation. It means that we can transmit a lot of information with gestures alone, without having to talk. However, if we can employ proper gestures while conversing with others, it will undoubtedly add spice to our conversation because words alone do not always suffice to convey thoughts. Our predecessors utilised gestures to communicate in the past, and spoken language arose only as their ability to manage their vocalisations developed.

According to an article by Olivia Mitchell – 'The three benefits of gesturing – it's not what you think'.

Gestures are a part of normal conversation. In normal conversation, our hands are probably gesturing without giving us any conscious thought. There is a theory that gestures were the precursor to language – **the gestural theory of language evolution.**

According to the gestural theory of language evolution, our ancestors were able to communicate intentionally through gestures but could not control their vocalisations. Therefore, they primarily used gestures to communicate purposefully; spoken language only began to emerge from this primarily gestural form of communication as our ancestors' ability to control their vocalisations increased. There are many theories given by researchers on gestures and their pre-existence. Gestural theories of language evolution contrast with competing theories that argue that because human language is now predominantly communicated by vocalisations, it is more reasonable to suppose that language developed from simpler kinds of primate vocal communication, such as song.

Current evidence suggests that gestural and vocal theories of language evolution are not incompatible. In fact, both may be more accurate when combined into a multimodal theory of language evolution, wherein human language evolved from, and continues to utilise, mutually informative gestures and vocalisations.[8]

An article on the neuroscience of dancing appeared in the June 2008 issue of Scientific American. Broca's region (the portion of the brain linked with speech production) is also stimulated during certain movement tasks, according to the study. As a result, it appears that **speaking and gestures** are inextricably linked.

But for some people, when they speak in front of a group, their natural gesturing disappears. According to Olivia Mitchell, people who had been talking with lots of gestures in the one-on-one rehearsal suddenly seem to lose that ability when they speak in front of a larger group. That is because a common reaction to being on show in front of a group is to freeze and become stiff – it is a symptom of nervousness. [9]

But practising the same can reduce anxiety and nervousness when speaking in public. Arts, especially dramatics, can be very helpful in removing this nervousness. Acting, singing, and poetry are the forms of art that help you create art products, be it an act on stage, a music performance, or a poem. And when you create such products, you showcase your talented product on stage or on-screen, and frequently doing this will help you to win over your nervousness, and sooner you will gain confidence to showcase your every gesture while communicating publicly on stage or while giving any sort of presentation in front of many people.

In Italy, body language is the most important part of making your point. The shrug of a shoulder, the flip of a wrist, or the lift of an eyebrow says more than a Sacco di parole (sack of words). Hand gestures are to Italian conversation what punctuation is to writing. Hands become exclamation points, periods, commas, and question marks. Italian gestures are a huge part of what makes an Italian, well, an ITALIAN!

Even before the law banned talking on cell phones while driving, Italians would pull over to the side of the road because they could not drive and carry on a conversation. In the old days of telephone booths, Italians would step outside so they would have space to express themselves fully.

It means gestures play a very important role in communication. They are like add-on features to speaking.

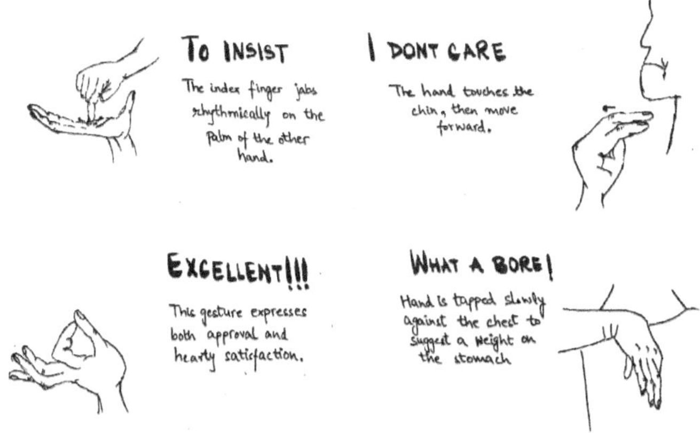

Here I want to share some of my experiences with dramatics and the role it played in improving my gestures. Dramatics not only help in gaining confidence in your gestures but also provide an opportunity to polish them.

In dramatics, if you are involved in performing some play as an actor or actress, then you must express yourself according to the need of the character that you are portraying. To portray someone, we have to rehearse a lot, notice very minute details of that character, and try to express that in the best way. And that improves the gestures of our body in day-to-day life too. Let me walk you through my journey of dramatics.

First time I performed on stage in front of the crowd, I was in 1st class. I was nervous. My feet were trembling, I could hear my heartbeat, but despite all of this, I performed. I do not know how well it went, but that gave me some confidence and I started participating.

After completing my 12th, I moved to college and here also I joined the dramatics club and participated in the 'Nukkad Natak' (Street Show). In the street show, there are so many gestures that we must learn to engage the audience. So, I learned a lot of them, and eventually, I realised that I have started using some gestures naturally while speaking. My continuous involvement in such activities helped me to overcome my nervousness while speaking and using my hand gestures in front of an unknown public.

I remember my trip to one of the hill stations in Himachal Pradesh with my friends. I was talking to one of my friends and suddenly he asked, "Do you do it intentionally?"

Me: What do I do?

Friend: All the gestures you use while speaking. Whatever you speak, there are a lot of gestures to explain each and everything.

Me: No, I don't do it intentionally. This is natural to me. Is it not good? Should I pay attention while speaking and should stop doing this?

Friend: No, no, not at all. It looks great. I love the way you do it. I also want to do it. I tried, but that is not natural to me.

Then I realised that some little gestures make you more appealing. You always get an edge over others while speaking or convincing someone. And dramatics or similar types of Arts play a very important role in improving it.

Previously, we understood how Arts help us in improving our gestures while communicating with others. Now, let us understand the benefits of gestures in the real world.

Gesturing helps you to be fluent and articulate. There is a large body of scientific evidence to support this. In an interesting study, three groups of subjects were asked to speak under different conditions. One group had both arms immobilised, the second group had one arm immobilised, and the third group was free to gesture. The experimenters found that disfluency increased as gesture was restricted. In addition, research shows that restricting hand gestures makes it more difficult to find the right words.

Gesturing conveys enthusiasm and energy to your audience. Surveys of what people like and dislike about presentations consistently report that people want presenters to show passion and enthusiasm.

Thirdly, when the audience sees you gesturing, they will think that you look confident. That is because nervous speakers are often frozen and stiff. Not only that, but you may also fool your mind into thinking you are confident. You will realise that you are speaking in a confident, conversational manner and start to feel that way too.[8]

In this era of Science, Technology, High level Engineering, creative business, and Digitalisation, effective communication is very necessary to convey your thoughts to the public. Communication is a skill that is a collection of many other soft skills, one of them is gesticulation. Gestures add glitter to the information we are communicating. And sometimes, when you are explaining some theories or ideas to others, words are just not enough to convey the exact information. Sometimes the person next to you may not be aware of the scientific or technical terms you are using; then gestures can only save you.

Any form of art, be it rapping, music composition, or acting, helps in gaining a good command over gestures involuntarily. Practising these art forms on a regular basis will surely help you become an effective communicator.

Public Speaking

As discussed previously, before humans started speaking, they used gestures to convey their thoughts. But gradually, we learned how to speak. At present, we all know how to put the words correctly so that they make some sense, i.e., we all know how to convey our thoughts by speaking.

Every day we speak to many people, or we talk to our friends, family members, and others. We are not afraid of communicating with the people who are in our close vicinity. We do not think twice while saying or explaining anything too familiar to people. But if we have to explain something in front of a group, especially if that group includes some of our well-known folks, we lose confidence, a worry arises from within, and we feel uneasy. We know the words, we know how to speak, we know how to talk with people, but still, we do not dare to speak in public or in front of a group. So how can we gain confidence? Is there any way to improve this skill?

Before that, let us understand what public speaking means.

It is a presentation that is given live before an audience. Public speeches can cover a wide variety of different topics. The goal of the speech may be to educate, entertain, or influence the listeners. Often, visual aids in the form of an electronic slideshow are used to supplement the speech. This makes it more attractive to the listeners.[10].

By definition, it is clear that – Public speaking is a way to deliver your ideas, thoughts, or reports in front of a public that may be of known individuals or unknown ones. Public speaking can be done using some tools as well, such as creative Arts, quiz polls, or electronic slideshows. Here, creativity plays an important role, so we can say that creativity can be integrated with your speaking skills to present your thoughts in public.

As long as there have been people, there has almost certainly been a public speech in some form or another. However, the origins of modern public speaking may be traced back to ancient Greece and Rome, according to most public speaking professionals working in commercial communication. Of course, there were no slide shows to assist in public speaking in those societies. They did, however, feel a need to talk in public. They created public speaking techniques as a result, which are still studied today.

The primary purpose of public speaking in ancient Greece was to praise or persuade others. All Greek citizens had the right to propose or oppose laws during their assembly at one time. This necessitated the hiring of professional public speakers. Speaking in front of a group of people became a coveted ability that was taught. Rhetoric was the term used by the Greeks to describe public speaking. Speaking in public was later employed in the Roman senate sessions once Rome rose to power. The Greeks' public speaking rhetoric was adopted by the Romans. In reality, at that time, the majority of public speaking instructors were Greek[10].

There are a lot of incidents that can be traced back in history related to public speaking. Continuous research in the field has evolved the concept of public speaking. As stated, Romans used to teach young students about this skill, and presently there are a lot of ways to improve the skill. One of them is practising dramatics. Let us take it step by step and understand the similarities between an actor and a speaker. Ginger, a leadership communications company that specialises in spoken-word situations, has beautifully described it on their blog. I have taken many references from their article to explain how dramatics help in enhancing public speaking.

Before a performance, both the actor and the public speaker must learn to control their stress and anxiety. Many people are surprised to learn that using your diaphragm as a stress reliever is quite helpful. Many people suffer from both public speaking and presentation anxiety. Nightmares such as missing lines, botching PowerPoint slides, misplacing notes, or stumbling over phrases can cause some people to wake up howling in the middle of the night. The truth is, becoming a courageous public speaker isn't about getting rid of or concealing your fear. It's all about turning that dread into exhilaration and enthusiasm. With basic relaxation techniques or basic breathing exercises, you can considerably reduce your worry.

Actors and speakers who are good at what they do don't act; they don't pretend to be someone they aren't. Both of them must be genuine and present their actual selves to the audience. The ability to be yourself in front of an audience is referred to as charisma and magnetism, or "presence." When giving a presentation, you must become accustomed to being in the spotlight—accepting your central role (and the exposure that comes with it) as a speaker entails accepting your central role (and the exposure that comes with it). You can tell that some presenters are uncomfortable with that degree of scrutiny. However, public speaking is a sort of performance. You won't be able to communicate your message with the world unless you are comfortable on stage!

Body language is an important aspect of public speaking. But mastering body language isn't about memorising a set of rules for where your arms and feet should be at any given time. Your body language is a reflection of your inner power, and it all starts with your mindset. "Attitude is a small thing that makes a tremendous difference," Winston Churchill stated. It should come as no surprise that how you handle yourself when giving a public speech has a significant impact on your audience.

Dramatics can teach a lot about it. Whenever we play a role in dramatics, we try to adopt the style of a character. For example, suppose you have to play the role of a lawyer in a play. In that case, you try to read about the lawyers, try to observe their talking style, their way of delivery, and their body language if it appeals to you. And suppose you practice a lot with the character. In that case, you tend to develop body language similar to that character, and involuntarily, you enhance your true self. If you get time, try experimenting with it.

Every actor and public speaker knows how to express themselves. Expressions play a heart-winning role in convincing your audience. Whenever you are speaking to the public, the first thing people see is your expression.

A good speaker realises that appropriate facial expressions are an important part of effective communication. Facial expressions are often the key determinant of the meaning behind the message.

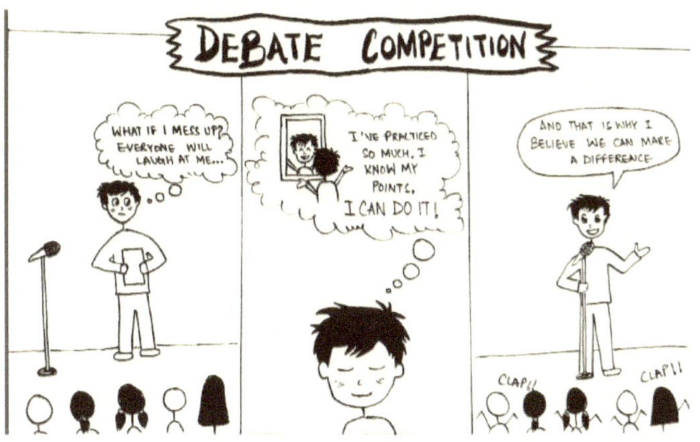

When we speak, our face tells more clearly than any other part of our body about our attitude, feelings, and emotions. Most of the time, we underrate the importance of facial expressions, but they play an important role in convincing the speaker and the message. The human face is thought to be capable of more than 10,000 different expressions using all of the muscles that accurately govern the mouth, lips, eyes, nose, forehead, and jaw. There are seven universally recognised emotions shown through facial expressions: anger, disgust, contempt, fear, happiness, sadness, and surprise. Regardless of culture, these expressions are the same all over the world. [11]

Practising dramatics can be a lot of fun and can help you comprehend and control these general expressions involuntarily.

When we play any character on stage, we have to show these different expressions to the public to convince them of the message. The same goes for the speaker. Consider, for example, if you have to give a college presentation or a presentation in your firm or a small presentation in school. Your idea of the presentation is related to water scarcity; you would try to keep your expression more inclined towards fear and sadness to convince your audience with your message.

The gestures are also important to add glitter to your information when presenting something to the people, as discussed previously.

In this era of technology, business, startups, your public speaking skills must be top-notch to convince your mentor, company professionals, or investors with your idea you want to implement or the strategy you want to follow to achieve any task.

Here, we understood how dramatics could help us present the idea or thought in the best possible way to the audience with the help of expressions, body language, or gestures. Still, these things do not work unless you get the confidence to stand in front of the public.

When we play a role in front of people, we gain some confidence in speaking and presenting ourselves to a group. If you've ever taken part in a play, you know how much effort is required when it's our first time. Our feet start trembling, our voice shivers, and our heartbeat quickens, but if we can get through the first play, we'll be a bit better prepared for the second. And if this continues, then there comes a day when we do not bother about our performance, our feet do not tremble, our heartbeat is normal, our voice does not shiver because we have that much confidence.

Similarly, if you are a singer or play any instrument, you will think to show your talent to the people one day or another. But here also, you will struggle the first time. As soon as that hurdle is crossed, you will feel some confidence, and upcoming days will give you more experience, and that will lead to more confidence. So basically, confidence is the key for anything, but that comes from experience, and experience is a collection of small steps to achieve something. That means we have to start first, and that is the hardest part of any goal.

Sometimes we begin, put in our best efforts for a few days, and then abandon the project. We feel awful when we set an unrealistic schedule to follow and don't meet nearly all of our expectations. It causes us to not only abandon that aim but also to lose confidence in our ability to take action in the future.

Have you ever considered why we are so terrified of speaking in front of a crowd? Let me tell you what goes through our heads when we are about to say something in front of a group of people. What if I make a mistake? What if the material I'm going to speak about isn't good enough? How will others assess me? What if I get stuck somewhere? What if I forget some words? And so on. Now let us imagine you are the audience, and some other person is speaking in front of you. Will you judge that person? Even if the speaker is not very good, are you going to tell him/her that you were not very great at delivering your content? My answer to this question will be no. Because most of the time, it does not matter for us. We are more concerned with what other people will think, but in reality, no one will think about yourself because they have their problems. Even if they judge you, let them judge, let them think. It should not bother you.

Some students are very shy to speak in public. They are full of thoughts before coming on stage. But practising drama just removes all this shyness. In theatre, there is a lot of rehearsal before giving the final shot. In my drama club, we used to interact daily with all the people because a play requires many crew members, and at some point, we must interact with them. So, in this process, we get to learn to interact at least with some people. Suppose we are consistent in this. This experience would be invaluable, and it can boost a lot of our confidence. In my college days also, I was regular in dramatic activities.

So, art is not only a part-time hobby. It improves you a lot. It makes you a different person. It gives you an edge over the others that are not involved in such types of activities. And public speaking is also a by-product of this. You do not have to pay to learn this. You just have to enjoy the process.

People Skill and Social Skill

Starting with an event I saw on LinkedIn about a 23-year-old man who was absolutely lost with his career path after his undergraduate since he was uninformed of his life in that particular sector after a certain period, the growth, and the type of job he would experience. In this predicament, he began using social media to contact people from other fields of study in order to figure out the best option.

Now you might be wondering how this incident is related to the mentioned chapter. People skills here play a crucial role in connecting with people physically or digitally.

Let us first take a look at the definition of people skills,

Neil Thompson has worked in this field and also wrote a book on people skills in 1996. Neil Thompson is a highly respected writer, teacher, and adviser, with over 40 years of experience in the people professions. He has held full or honorary professorships at four UK universities. He is now a sought-after trainer, consultant, and conference speaker.

According to Neil Thompson, People skills are patterns of behaviour and behavioural interactions. It is an umbrella term for skills under three related sets of abilities: **personal effectiveness, interaction skills, and mediation.**

Personal effectiveness is all about how you come across to others. Are you able to pitch yourself? Can you communicate clearly? Can you get what you need from others? Someone with strong personal effectiveness typically also makes a memorable first impression and has a confident presence with the people they meet.

Interaction ability can be defined as how you predict and decode behaviour. In an interaction, can you empathize with someone? Are you highly perceptive?

Intercession is the ability to lead, influence, and build bridges between people. Are you a connector? A mediator? Often this can involve calming down difficult or toxic people. [12]

In general terms, people skills are a kind of tool that we use to communicate effectively and interact effectively with others, understand others, and convince others. This skill or tool is a gift to human beings to convey emotions and thoughts to another person without hurting others' emotions. If we look deep, this skill can be inherited or acquired in various ways, by taking online lectures, courses, but what I have experienced and many others involved in co-curricular activities, like Dramatics, is that they were able to acquire this tool via practising Dramatics.

Here, I will share some of my experiences that relate to how Dramatics have helped me work on this skill.

Any group activity like working on skits, plays, or technical projects gives us a chance to interact with people. For example, when I worked on my research project, I connected with many people to pitch my idea or to ask them to help me find solutions to some of the problems associated with the project. Similarly, dramatics or any other art form, be it rapping, have also provided me many opportunities to interact with various people with various interests like directing, writing, music production, etcetera, and with continuous practice of interacting with these people, helped me to become habitual in interacting with people in a friendly manner and also helped me in understanding people's behaviour. By regularly practicing and experimenting with your style of speaking, language, gestures, you soon evolve with good people skills.

Dramatics give us a chance to play roles of various characters and give us opportunities to understand and observe various characters deeply. If you learn from these observations and try to use your learnings in real life, your goal may succeed. For example, I once watched and observed a good YouTube video of a person bargaining with a fruit seller on a roadside. The kind of tone and attitude he used was so much acceptable to that seller that he quickly dropped down the price of the fruits. I once experimented with this act. Initially, I was unable to get the results that I wanted, but soon that strategy worked.

Understanding characters is the best way to understand the person you are talking with. Suppose you observe the characteristics and behaviour of a person. In that case, it becomes very easy for you to convey your thoughts.

Dramatics allow us to deeply understand the characters by observing every minute detail, which ultimately helps us to work better on our **personal effectiveness (how you have to present yourself), Interaction ability (how we have to speak) and Intercession ability (what we have to speak).**

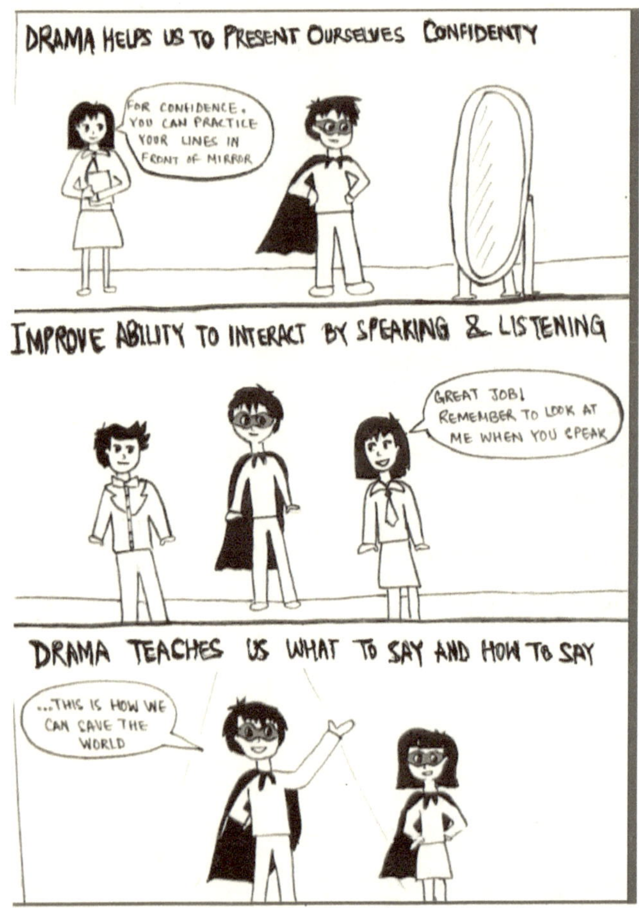

People skills are based on this simple phenomenon only. So, in short, it can be concluded that dramatics give us a chance to observe various characters. This practice improves our power of observing real human beings. This observation and understanding will ultimately help to convince people easily.

Forbes mentioned 20 people's skills to succeed in life. They are **Ability to relate with others, Strong communication skills, Patience with others, Trusting others, Active listening skills, genuine interest in others, Flexibility, knowing how and when to empathise, Good judgement, Ability to persuade others, Negotiation skills, Ability to keep an open mind, A great sense of humour, Knowing your audience, Honesty, Awareness of body language, Proactive problem-solving, Leadership skills, Good manners, Ability to motivate others.**

Most of these skills can be acquired by practising dramatics passionately, as explained in previous chapters.

Now let us explore another soft skill, similar to people skills. Social skill is another tool that works similarly. Still, there is a little bit of difference between the two. People skills are more dominant when we work with people on professional terms. Social skill is dominant when we interact with people on emotional terms.

Let me explain this thing with an example. I worked on a video project named Ehsaas, a rap track on the life of a broken criminal. I worked on the video with some of my friends. I wanted to work with them. Those people were skilled in their work, and I had no other resources to complete my work professionally.

Without social skills, this task would have been impossible, as we were all working on the project for free. Convincing my friends to complete the work on time was difficult. Here, my social connection with them and my understanding of them on the social front worked crucially to convince them of my idea and vision for the project. This can be categorised as my social skill, which helped me work in a team with them and guide them in the process.

If we work on a project in a team, we first connect and talk with people to understand the vision and the problem. Then we talk with people to understand the function. In the end, we connect and talk with people to present our solution.

Whether we work professionally or work emotionally, the people's skills and social skills are important tools in conveying thoughts most efficiently and convincing people in the most amazing style.

Many research papers and articles on the internet emphasise the importance of Arts, Theatre, Music, and Dramatics in general in the development of future leaders and professionals. In one of the chapters, "Social Skills Outcomes of Art Education" from the e-book Art for Art's Sake? The Impact of Arts Education by the Organisation for Economic Co-operation and Development (OECD), there are many examples related to the same. I am sharing some of them for your reference.

In July 2010, 50 World Economic Forum fellows travelled to Columbia University in New York to explore how theatre may help them become future leaders of countries or businesses. The programme aims to teach fellows how performers captivate their audience's attention and influence their view. The idea was also to encourage people to express themselves via their body rather than simply words. One of the activities offered to these potential leaders was to act like an oppressed person and improvise a discussion. After the lesson, one of the participants stated that the activities had given him some space to consider other people's motives. He continued, "knowing ourselves and expressing our opinions" was the goal.

Social skills play an important role in all age groups and professions, especially professions associated with Science and Technology. The importance of social skills for students is to express their ideas and grow comfortable and confident with a wide variety of materials and modes of expression and connect with other people in meaningful and productive ways. When it comes to professionals in any business, social skills are important to carry out work in the most efficient way and in the least time. In areas of research, Science, and technology, social skills play a very important role in converting your ideas into meaningful business by continuously interacting with people.

Finally, I'd like to state that the arts play a vital role in the development of an individual's total personality. A person's perspective is altered through the arts. It inadvertently improves a variety of soft skills, such as social skills, people skills, creativity, and so on, all of which are intertwined.

Today, in the 21st century, where jobs are very few in a country like India, India is a country that has a good GDP. However, when it comes to GDP per capita, we are not standing anywhere to compete with other nations such as China. The only way to create more GDP per capita is to create more innovative solutions to the problems pertaining to the root level.

Social skill, in general, is very important to understand the problems existing in society at different levels and areas. Social skill helps you to make friends with people, creating change at different levels. It helps you understand the person sitting next to you and provide him with a good solution.

That problem can be very small or so crucial that it could be the next billion-dollar idea.

Research and Development

Research and development (R&D) is a way to create new or improved technology that can provide a competitive advantage at the business, industry, or national level. [13].

Research is a risky task, as it can take several years to conclude or maybe after much time spending the research is stopped by the company if it is not yielding fruitful results. At the same time, if the idea succeeds, it might be a huge success for the organisation.

The majority of R&D projects do not produce the promised financial results, and the successful projects (25 to 50 per cent) must pay for the unsuccessful or prematurely ended ones. Furthermore, the innovator of R&D cannot keep all of the benefits of its breakthroughs to themselves; they must share them with customers, the general public, and even competitors. As a result, a company's Research and Development operations must be meticulously structured, controlled, assessed, and managed. [13]

The goal of academic and institutional R&D is to gain new knowledge that can be transferred to practical applications. Industrial R&D, on the other hand, aims to achieve further information that may be applied to a company's commercial demands and eventually lead to new or enhanced goods, processes, systems, or services that can boost sales and profitability.

Basic Research, Applied Research, and development are the three forms of R&D defined by the National Science Foundation (NSF). The goal of basic research is to

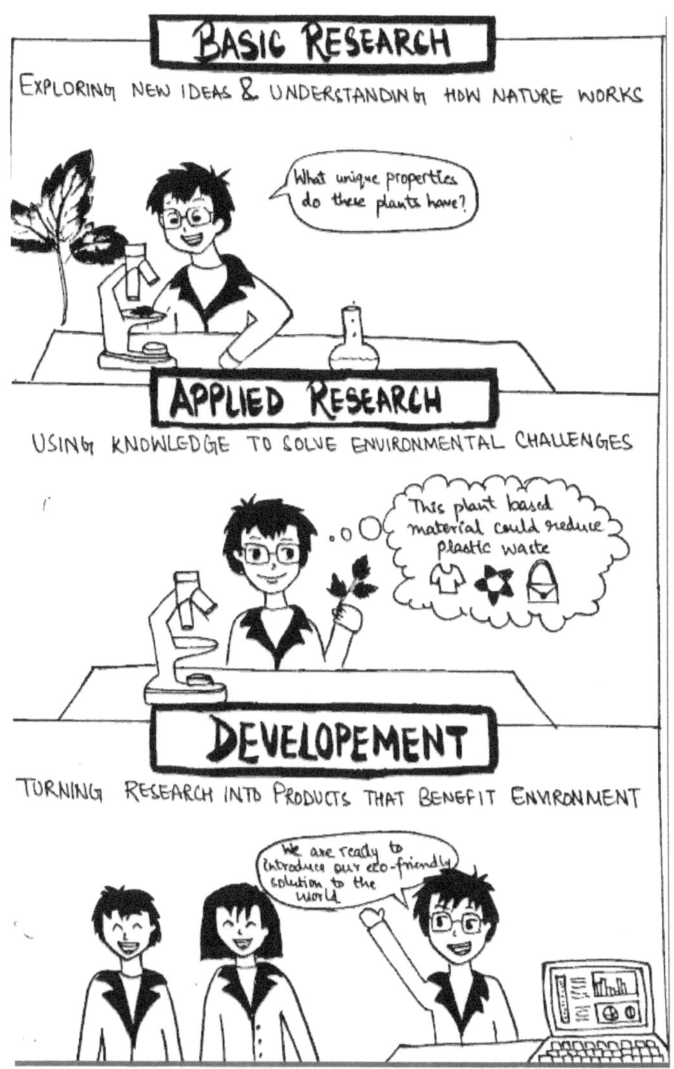

Understand the issue under study better rather than to use it in a practical way. Basic Research, as applied to the industrial sector, is defined as research that enhances scientific knowledge but has no explicit commercial goal, even if the investigation is in domains of current or potential importance to the company.

Applied Research is focused on getting the knowledge or understanding needed to determine the best way to meet a recognised and specific need. Applied Research refers to investigations aimed at discovering new knowledge with specific commercial goals in terms of products, processes, or services in the business world. The systematic application of scientific knowledge or understanding towards the manufacture of valuable materials, technologies, systems, or procedures, including the design and development of prototypes and processes, is known as development.

It's critical to distinguish development from Engineering at this time. Engineering is the application of cutting-edge knowledge to the design and manufacture of commercially viable products. Research generates knowledge, whereas development makes prototypes and tests their viability. Engineering transforms these prototypes into marketable items or processes used to manufacture commercial goods and services. [13].

All the industries spend a considerable amount on Research and Development. Industries can be automotive, computing and electronics, health care, software. Companies like Amazon, Alphabet, Volkswagen, and

Honda are among the top 50 companies that spend a lot on R&D.

R&D is the backbone of these industries because, without R&D, new products can't be developed. R&D is one of the secure jobs to take.

India has emerged as the preferred place for cutting-edge Research and Development (R&D) projects for global firms across industries, according to an article published in 2019 by India Briefing.

Companies in the information technology (IT), car, pharmaceutical, telecommunications, and other sectors have established captive technology centres to boost R&D in areas such as the Internet of Things (IoT), artificial intelligence, and data analytics.

OnePlus, a Chinese smartphone manufacturer, announced plans to construct its first R&D centre in India in Hyderabad in 2018. Oppo, another Chinese smartphone manufacturer, established its R&D centre in India on December 15, 2018, intending to make it the company's largest outside of China.

Foxconn, a Taiwanese multinational electronics contract manufacturing behemoth with manufacturing plants in Andhra Pradesh and Tamil Nadu, has chosen Hyderabad as its advanced industrial artificial intelligence R&D centre. Meanwhile, Lotte Group, a Korean retail behemoth, is establishing an R&D facility in India to support its digital campaign and international expansion.

In the automotive industry, Volkswagen has launched a new R&D centre in Pune. Nissan Motors has inked an MoU with the Kerala state government to establish its first global centre for digital operations in Thiruvananthapuram.

Microsoft, Intel, Nokia, Motorola, HP, Oracle, IBM, SAP, and Cisco are among the IT behemoths with established R&D facilities in India. Aside from these, more than 100 Fortune 500 businesses have opened R&D centres in India, including Delphi, Eli Lilly, General Electric, Hewlett Packard, and DaimlerChrysler.

For corporations establishing R&D centres in India, India provides a unique combination of extensive market opportunity, technical skills, cost-effectiveness, aggressive government backing, and highly scalable and low-cost labour. Every year, India produces a large number of Engineering and Science graduates. Choosing graduates from the top 15% of institutions still amounts to tens of thousands of promising applicants, although labour quality varies greatly. The availability of this workforce at a reasonable cost is what sets India apart from other countries. Hiring a researcher in India, for example, costs one-fifth of what it does in the United States. [14]

Global behemoths like Google, Microsoft, SAP, and IBM have announced plans to invest in and incubate startups and engage with tiny early-stage service providers through venture funds, evangelist programmes, and alliances, all to solve consumer problems faster. These businesses have discovered that startups are the most efficient in developing a product and bringing it to market.

Collaboration with startups can assist MNCs in mitigating risks, reducing time to market, and lowering costs. Furthermore, such alliances open up a wide range of opportunities for stakeholders to innovate and produce value.

India's startup ecosystem is third only to the US and the UK. According to industry reports, the number of startups in the country has gone up from 7,000 in 2008 to 50,000 in 2018. [14]

It is clear from the above-stated facts that there will be various job opportunities in Research and Development in India in the coming years. There will be a lot of encouragement by multiple companies and the government on establishing and funding startups.

And as the job opportunities increase, the competition in the market also increases. The future generation must be ready with the suitable skill set needed to become a good professional in Research and development. The scope of R&D in a different field is different, and the kind of technical skills required to survive in R&D in different areas will be different. For example, in the automotive industry, the technical skills required will be more mechanical or electrical oriented. In the software industry, the skill would be more oriented to computer applications and coding. Similarly, in telecommunications and chip development, the technical skills would be more inclined towards electronics.

The set of soft skills required for a sound Research and Development engineer, or manager, is more or less the same in all the fields. The vision of STEM is to teach various multidisciplinary technical and analytical skills to students. The concept of STEAM is to integrate Arts with specialised technical knowledge to provide multiple soft skills to students such as empathy, leadership, teamwork, people skills, social skills, and creativity. To be good in R&D, a person must be equipped with all sorts of soft skills and technical skills to create remarkable inventions in the future to serve the company and the nation.

This book is written to help students, teachers of schools, parents, and professors in college understand the vision of STEAM and the purpose of multidisciplinary learning for the students.

The colleges and schools situated in India are different concerning their infrastructure, faculty, and other resources. So, the curriculum of STEAM that must be implemented in these institutions will be diverse. Now, it is up to the institutions how they will be adopting the STEAM philosophy. The institution can promote group activities associated with Arts, be it music, dance, poetry, storytelling, etcetera, and each student in college or school must understand that these are not just hobbies but are essential subjects in overall development. Parents must encourage their children to take any of the art forms as their hobby from childhood because the foundation created will guide the future of their children. I'm not suggesting that parents force this information on their children from an early age. This will place a significant amount of strain on them and their children. I believe in exposing children to a variety of STEAM subjects at a young age and allowing them to choose an appropriate Arts subject for the rest of their lives, as well as allowing them to combine whatever other courses they study in the future with arts.

References

1. Towards More Effective Education: Emergence of STEM Education in India by Vivekananda International Foundation

2. https://www.childdrama.com/

3. UK essays.

4. medium.com blog.

5. https://www.verywellmind.com/what-is-cognition

6. https://www.trainingjournal.com/blog/near-and-far-transfer-learning.

7. https://www.edutopia.org/blog/7-leadership-skills-fostered-arts-education-stacey-goodman

8. https://www.researchgate.net/publication/315334354_Gestural_Theory_of_Language_Evolution

9. https://speakingaboutpresenting.com/delivery/the-three-benefits-of-gesturing/

10. https://business.tutsplus.com/tutorials/what-is-public-speaking--cms-31255

11. https://www.karstennoack.com/facial-expressions-public-speaking/

12. https://www.Scienceofpeople.com/people-skills/

13. https://www.inc.com/encyclopedia/research-and-development.html

14. https://www.india-briefing.com/news/rd-in-india-18919.html/